Mommy's Disease: Helping Children Understand Alcoholism

Book 2 of the Helping Children Understand Series

Other books by Carolyn Hannan Bell:

Daddy's Disease: Helping Children Understand Alcoholism

Illustrations by PeiPei

Copyright 2014 by Carolyn Hannan Bell. All rights reserved worldwide. No part of this publication may be replicated, redistributed, or given away in any form without the prior written consent of the author/publisher or the terms relayed to you herein.

This is a work of fiction. Names, characters, businesses, places, events and incidents are either the products of the author's imagination or used in a fictitious manner. Any resemblance to actual persons, living or dead, or actual events is purely coincidental.

ISBN-13: 978-1495984181 * ISBN-10: 1495984184

For Ron who teaches about serenity every day.

Thank you, Alex, for helping your technologically challenged mother and for teaching me to do a proper push-up and much gratitude to my favorite family: Mom, Pop, Jacqui, Will, Alex and Ron for your meticulous editing, constant support and for loving me so well.

Once upon a time, a girl named Mila lived in a nice home with her Mom and Dad and her dog, Annie. There were family dinners, movie nights and dress-up tea parties, and all was well until Mommy started to change. She fell asleep on the couch a lot, sometimes even on the floor. She didn't make dinner like she used to, or meet Mila at the bus stop after school, and when she did, she was acting strangely—she talked funny and bumped into things. Mommy and Daddy started to argue, and sometimes they yelled at each other. Mommy didn't play with Mila so much and didn't even seem to want to spend time with her. Mila didn't understand what she had done wrong.

Now Mila's parents don't live together anymore. Mila lives with her Dad and her dog, Annie, and she misses her Mom a lot. Mila and her Mom are scheduled to see each other every week, but sometimes her Mom doesn't show up when she's supposed to.

It was six-fifteen on a Tuesday evening—only fifteen more minutes before her Mom was due to arrive to take Mila out to her favorite pizza place for dinner. She had been looking forward to this night for three whole days—just her and Mommy and as much pizza and orange soda as she wanted! Sometimes, fifteen minutes could seem like a month! Then fifteen minutes turned into twenty, and twenty turned into thirty, until it turned into time for Mila to go to bed.

Her Mom never came and Mila didn't know why.

Annie jumped right into bed with Mila and tried her best to cheer her up with kisses and cuddles. But Mila was too sad.

Daddy came into the room and sat on the edge of Mila's bed and wiped her tears.

"Mom promised she'd be here. Why doesn't Mommy want to be with me? Why doesn't she love me? What did I do wrong?" Mila cried.

Dad held Mila close and stroked her hair. "Mommy loves you very much. You didn't do anything at all to keep her from coming tonight."

Mila buried her head under the covers and Annie followed right in after her.

Dad peeked under the blanket at Mila and gently explained. "What happened tonight didn't have anything to do with how much Mommy loves you. The reason she didn't come tonight is that she has a disease that makes her forget the things she promises you. It makes her act in ways that she's ashamed of."

"That's silly." said Mila.

Annie cocked her head and looked at Daddy as he explained.

"The disease is called alcoholism, and a person who has the disease is called an alcoholic. Mommy is an alcoholic."

Mila was too tired and too sad to talk anymore that night, so she cuddled up next to Annie and went to sleep.

Something weird happened at school that week. Mila's best friend, Jackie, was home sick all week with chicken pox.

Mr. Bogan, her teacher, explained to the class that chicken pox is a disease that causes itchy bumps and is really easy to catch.

Mila missed Jackie a lot, and she wished she would come back to school and play with her. Instead, she played with her other good buddies Karin and Christie. Together, they made a get well card to help Jackie feel better.

As Mila was walking home from school she started to think about what her Dad had said about her mother's disease, and she wondered if it was like Jackie's disease. As soon as she got home, she told her Dad about Jackie's chicken pox.

"Jackie has chicken pox, and she had to stay home so the other kids wouldn't catch it. Is Mommy's disease like chicken pox?" asked Mila.

"Well," answered Daddy, "There are some things that chicken pox and alcoholism have in common. The first thing is that it's nobody's fault when someone gets either disease."

Mila nodded her head and said, "Yeah, you can't help it if you get sick!"

"Right," answered Dad, "and when you have chicken pox your skin feels really itchy and it's very hard not to scratch. But if you scratch you could get some pretty icky scars, so you have to try really hard not to scratch."

"Does Mommy itch?" interrupted Mila.

"No, Honey. Mommy doesn't have chicken pox—she has alcoholism. It's not itchy, but in the same way it's hard not to scratch an itchy chicken pox, it's really hard for Mom not to drink alcohol."

"So, Mommy has a disease that makes her really thirsty?"

Annie licked her lips.

"Not exactly," explained Daddy. Mila was getting confused.

"Alcoholism makes Mommy's body have a kind of allergy to beer, wine and liquor, which are all types of alcohol. When she drinks alcohol it's hard for her to stop and then the alcohol affects how she thinks, feels and behaves."

"It's kind of like your allergy. Do you remember what happens to you when you eat peanuts?" Mila thought for a moment, and said, "Like the time when I ate that cookie with peanut butter in it and it made me not able to breathe?"

"Exactly," said Daddy. "There isn't anything you can do to make yourself not be allergic to peanuts, right?"

"Yeah, so I just don't even eat peanuts 'cause I never want not to be able to breathe again!"

Annie thumped her tail and licked Mila's cheek.

"How come Mommy keeps drinking alcohol when it makes her act in bad ways? Why doesn't she stop drinking alcohol like I stopped eating peanuts?"

Dad thought for a bit and said slowly, "It's kind of difficult to explain. Mommy's disease makes her crave alcohol. That means that her body feels like it really wants alcohol. It's like a voice inside her says 'have a drink—it will taste sooooo good, and you will feel sooooo much better.'"

"A voice inside her brain that tells her to do things?" Mila questioned.

"Well, it can be a voice or a really strong feeling that nags at her all day and all night long and it doesn't stop until she takes a drink. Once she takes even one drink, it's very, very hard for her to stop drinking until she falls really deeply asleep."

Mila felt confused and tried to understand what Daddy was saying. Finally, she looked up at him and said, "I don't understand that."

Annie rolled over on her back so that Mila would scratch her belly. She was getting pretty confused by all of this too.

Mila had enough of this conversation and wanted to talk about her Halloween costume and trick-or-treating. Halloween was only one week away!

She couldn't decide if she was going to be a Princess, a Vampire, a Cowgirl or a Pirate, or…

Daddy said, "Why don't you think of your very favorite thing in the whole world and be that for Halloween?"

Annie nuzzled Mila's hand in agreement.

Mila looked at Daddy with a huge grin on her face and said, "I'm gonna be Annie for Halloween!!!"

It was the best Halloween ever! Jackie's chicken pox was all gone, so Mila went trick-or-treating with her, Karin and Christie. They stayed out for hours going from house to house and collecting more candy and goodies than they ever thought possible. Mila couldn't wait to get home and dump her treats on the kitchen table and dig in!

When she got home it was really late—almost eight o'clock at night. Daddy said that Mila could have two small pieces of candy before she got ready for bed. Mila felt very disappointed.

"Two? Come on, Dad! Puleeze, puleeze can I have just four, puleeze?" Annie thumped her tail in agreement.

"Candy will make it harder for you to get to sleep. Two is plenty and you can have more tomorrow." Daddy sounded really serious, so Mila ate her two pieces (it was hard to pick just two) and got ready for bed.

After Daddy tucked Mila and Annie into bed, they both felt restless and excited. They were thinking about how much fun they had trick-or-treating, but mostly they were thinking about all that delicious candy only a few steps away in the kitchen. They tossed and turned and tried really hard to squeeze their eyes closed, but it wasn't working. All they could think about was CANDY!!!!

So, Mila and Annie quietly slid out of bed and crept across the floor and down the stairs to the kitchen. They were very careful not to wake Daddy as they snuck past his bedroom door. They knew how upset he would be if he caught them, but they didn't seem to be able to help themselves.

Finally, they got to the kitchen and pulled the giant pillow case filled with candy onto the floor and dug in.

The chocolate and caramel and sweet and sour and soft and chewy and crunchy tastes were so yummy that they didn't think of anything else other than how good they felt.

They didn't even hear Daddy come into the kitchen.

Daddy was not happy.

Mila's face was smeared with chocolate and Annie's beard had sticky, gooey caramel stuck in it. Mila knew she was in big trouble, but the worst part was that Daddy didn't even yell at her.

He just looked so sad and told Mila how disappointed he was in her, which made her feel sad and ashamed.

She didn't like that feeling at all.

Daddy cleaned up their faces and made Mila brush her teeth for a really, really long time.

Then he put them both back in bed, turned out the light and closed the door. Mila felt just terrible about what she'd done.

And also kind of sick…

When Mila woke up the next morning, she could hear Daddy making breakfast in the kitchen. The thought of food made her stomach feel funny.

She was so sorry she had not listened to Daddy and had eaten all that candy. She felt awful, but it was a school day and Mila had to go to school.

Plus, today was her band concert and she had been looking forward to that for weeks!

After she dressed, she and Annie went downstairs—hoping that Daddy wasn't still mad at them. "Good morning, you two. How are you feeling today?" Daddy asked.

Mila didn't want to tell him the truth because she knew that it was her own fault she felt sick. "Okay," she said, but she really wasn't.

When she saw the waffles waiting for her at the table, her stomach hurt and her face turned green. Daddy sent her back to bed.

She was going to have to miss school, and playing her flute at the concert, and her friends, and it was her own fault.

Mila was so sad and disappointed that she couldn't sleep. After a while, Dad came in and sat on the edge of her bed, felt her forehead, and gave her a kiss.

Mila cried, "I'm so sorry I hurt your feelings by not doing what you told me."

Daddy answered, "This has nothing to do with my feelings. You weren't thinking about me when you ate that candy! But, maybe you can use this experience to understand Mommy's disease a little better."

"Huh?" asked Mila. Annie cocked her head.

"Well, you didn't eat that candy because you didn't love me enough, or because I wasn't being a good enough Dad—just like Mommy doesn't drink because she doesn't love you enough or think you aren't being a good enough daughter!"

Dad pulled Mila close to him and explained, "You know how impossible it was for you to have a whole pillow case filled with candy and only have one or two pieces? Remember how it felt like one, or two or even three pieces were not enough? And how that voice in your head kept telling you how good another piece of candy would taste? Remember how hard it was to think about anything else?

Well, that's kind of what it's like for Mommy or anyone else who has a drinking problem. The difference is that the voice inside Mommy's mind is there all the time—every day and every night. That's what makes it so hard for her not to have a drink. Once she starts drinking, it's even harder for her stop."

"I remember. But, I'm never gonna eat too much candy again. I feel so sick and I missed my concert at school! Maybe we should tell Mommy that she will feel sick from alcohol if she has more than one drink?"

"Mommy already knows that. She's the only one who can stop her drinking. She knows that she should stop. She knows that drinking will make her feel sick and make her miss things, but it's just so hard to stop once she starts. That's the disease part of alcoholism," explained Daddy. "An alcoholic can't stop after one or two or even seven drinks. Once she has one drink, she'll usually keep drinking until she falls asleep."

"So Mommy could just never drink again, and then she won't be an alcoholic anymore!" exclaimed Mila.

Dad smoothed Mila's sheets where Annie rumpled them and said, "No, alcoholism never goes away. But, an alcoholic can make the choice to stop drinking alcohol. There are special people who can help her learn how to stop. That's called 'being in recovery.'"

"So, that means that Mommy should never have a drink again? Not even one? Not ever?"

"That's exactly right, sweetie," said Daddy. Mila hugged Annie close and thought about all the things Dad was teaching her.

"So how come the alcohol makes her forget stuff and act mean sometimes?" asked Mila.

Daddy held Mila's hand and explained, "Alcohol affects your brain and makes you say or do things that you wouldn't normally do. It's a little bit like how you get when you're really sleepy or really hungry. You get grumpy and tired and it's hard for you to behave well."

After a few moments, Mila looked up at Dad and said angrily, "If Mommy really loved me then she would never drink alcohol at all. She wouldn't drink something that makes her say mean things, or yell, or forget to take me places. If she loved me…"

"Whoa! Whoa!" Daddy interrupted. "Mommy's drinking doesn't have a thing to do with you, or me or anyone or anything. She drinks because she chooses to drink, because of that voice inside her head and because she hasn't learned how not to drink."

Mila's eyes filled with tears as she said, "If Mommy loved me then she just wouldn't have any drinks at all!"

"Did you eat all that candy because you didn't love me?" asked Daddy. "Of course not—it's the same thing with Mommy's drinking."

Annie seemed to agree and began to chew on her favorite stuffed dragon.

Daddy hugged Mila tightly and kissed the top of her head.

"Your Mommy loves you more than anything in this whole world," he said. "It's this terrible disease, and nothing else, that makes her drink and it's the drinking that makes her behave badly. None of this has anything to do with you!"

"Do you remember all the ways your Mom has shown you how much she loves you? Like when she helped you sell Girl Scout cookies, made you dresses, and taught you how to make bracelets?"

Mila's eyes lit up, "Like when she took me to the American Girl Place in New York City and we looked at all those dolls?!"

Mila drifted to sleep with dreams of all the fun things she and Mommy had done together and how good she felt thinking of those fun times.

When Mila got up the next day, she realized it was Saturday and she could spend the morning watching cartoons, brushing Annie's hair and painting her toe nails.

She still felt tired from all the talking she and Dad did the night before. Talking about hard things, like Mommy's disease, took a lot of energy! She had to rest up for her afternoon play date with Jackie.

But, things didn't go so well with Jackie this time. Jackie really wanted to work on the mouse house they were building together, but Mila wanted to relax and watch "Brave" on television.

Mila was too tired and too upset to work things out with Jackie, so she called her Dad to come and pick her up early.

On the way home, Dad wanted to know what happened, but Mila didn't want to talk about it. Daddy reminded her how important it is to talk about feelings, especially hard feelings.

Mila exclaimed, "Jackie wouldn't do what I wanted and I was her guest!"

Dad thought for a moment and asked, "Did you try to work things out with her? Did you look for a compromise so you could both be happy?"

"No," answered Mila, "I didn't feel like talking to her. I was too mad!"

When they got home Dad let Mila watch "Brave" and calm down a bit. Then he came over to her on the couch and told her they needed to talk a bit about how important it is to work problems out. He told her that not talking about hard things is something that Mommy has trouble with too.

"I think that what happened today may help you understand Mommy's disease a bit more," said Dad.

Annie looked up from her dragon to hear what he had to say.

"Mommy drinks alcohol because it helps her to not think about her problems. It makes her forget about the hard or painful things in her life, like difficulties at work, or arguments she might be having with me. Unfortunately, it also makes her forget about the good and loving things in her life like you and the fun things that you and she do together. That's why Mommy often breaks her promises to you—the alcohol makes her forget that she ever made the promises in the first place!"

"You always tell me to talk about my problems," Mila said proudly.

Daddy put his arm around Mila and said, "That's a really good way to work on the things that are bothering you. But drinking and forgetting is Mommy's way of handling her problems. She drinks because the voice in her head tells her to drink, but also because it's the only way she really knows how to make her troubles and bad feelings go away."

"You mean if Mommy is sad or mad at something, she thinks that if she drinks some alcohol then she won't feel sad or mad anymore?" asked Mila.

"That's right," answered Dad, "but when she wakes up after being drunk, her problems are still there, and she still feels sad and mad and also ashamed for having gotten drunk again."

Mila looked up at Dad, "You mean that Mommy feels ashamed of drinking? What's 'drunk'?"

"'Drunk' is what happens to your body after you drink too much alcohol," said Daddy, "and yes, Mommy is very much ashamed when she gets drunk. She doesn't want to disappoint you or let you down. Each time she does, she feels worse about herself. But, she doesn't know any other way to deal with those feelings other than to try to make them go away with more drinking. It's a circle that just keeps spinning around."

Annie and Mila both groaned.

"Does that mean that she could still love me and be mean to me at the same time? She could love me and not show up at my soccer game or take me to dinner?"

"That's exactly right," Daddy answered. "She acts the way she does because of her drinking and never, ever because of her feelings for you. She drinks because she is sad and she is sad because she drinks."

"What if I were really, really good and didn't cause any problems?

What if I never asked Mommy to take me anywhere, and did all my homework and cleaned my room?

Then she wouldn't feel so sad or have any more problems and then she wouldn't have to drink!"

Dad took Mila's hand and said, "Oh Honey, you have to try to understand that Mommy doesn't drink because of anything you do or anything you don't do.

She drinks because she has a disease and because she hasn't figured out a way to not drink.

She loves you with all her heart and she always will.

There isn't anything that you could do, good or bad, that could, in any way, cause Mommy to drink."

"How could she figure out not to drink?" asked Mila.

"First," said Daddy, "Mommy has to want to stop drinking. She has to admit to herself that she has a problem and that she needs help to solve it. After that, there are really helpful groups like Alcoholics Anonymous that she could join. There are people there who could teach her ways to handle her problems and her feelings without drinking alcohol."

"Can we take her there? Maybe tomorrow?" asked Mila. Annie's tail thumped loudly on the bed.

"No, Honey. That's something Mommy has to do on her own. We didn't cause her drinking problem and we can't fix it. You can support her and cheer her on if she decides to get better, but until then, you have to protect your feelings."

"Protect my feelings from what?"

"Well," said Daddy, "it's not good for you to believe that you can make Mommy drink or not drink. When you think Mommy drinks because she doesn't love you enough to stop drinking, or that something you did caused her to drink—that's the same as thinking that everything she feels and does is because of you. That's simply not true. She loves you and she always will no matter what. You just have to remember that Mommy is in charge of herself. You can only be in charge of you."

"But if I never did anything bad wouldn't that make it easier for Mom to not drink?" asked Mila.

"One has nothing to do with the other. Even if everything were the best it could possibly be, Mommy would still drink. It isn't about what's going on around her—she drinks because of what's going on inside her. She doesn't know how not to drink, and nothing and no one can change that except her." Daddy explained.

"So what should I do?" asked Mila.

Dad put his arms around Mila and said, "You just keep being the wonderful, sweet little girl you are. Don't change a thing about yourself. Your job is to do your best to grow and to learn. That's what all of us are here to do!

Mommy will find her own way. All we can do is hope that she'll find a way that doesn't include alcohol. You just keep being the best you can be, and keep trying to understand that Mommy makes her own choices and that those choices aren't because of anything you do or don't do. She loves you with her whole heart, just like I do."

Annie licked Daddy right on the nose and Mila giggled.

"Mommy's disease may cause her to be mean to you, and that's where you may have to work the hardest—to keep thinking about what you've learned about alcoholism.

You have to work extra hard to remember that alcohol, and not you, is what makes Mommy behave badly. The way Mommy acts is not your fault."

Annie snuggled up onto Mila's pillow. Her favorite place to sleep was right next to Mila's face.

Mila leaned back on her pillow and closed her eyes. "I think I can sleep now, Daddy. I hope Mommy's okay, but I'm glad she's not mad at me."

Daddy gave Mila a kiss on the forehead and pulled her covers up snuggly to her chin.

"Goodnight, sweet girl," he said, "We'll keep talking about this and figuring things out as we go and all will be well.

I love you so much, always will, never won't."

And, he turned out the light to welcome Mila's sweet dreams.

Carolyn Hannan Bell is a practicing Psychotherapist in New Jersey. She works with families and individuals suffering from the emotional effects of alcohol and substance abuse. This is her second children's book.

PRAISE FOR *DADDY'S DISEASE*

"…absolutely wonderful. I have counseled so many kids who would have benefitted from this book."
Gail McVey, Psy.D., School Psychologist

"This is an important book in that it brings the shame and secrecy of alcoholism into an arena of understanding for children who often feel responsible for the actions of their parents. It is an excellent addition to this library's collection."
Karen Casaceli, M.Ed., M.L.I.S. School Library Media Specialist

"Carolyn's words in this book will gently encourage difficult conversations to begin while allowing the little one not to feel alone or unloved… what a powerful, transformative gift awaits the reader of this book. I highly recommend it."
Frances Schwabenland, M.S., M.Ed.

"The author clearly understands the mind of an alcoholic, and does a fine job explaining it in a simple, easy to understand manner. I was most surprised to find that the book, while geared towards children, explains alcoholism so simply yet so well that I find myself wishing that many adults in my life could read and grasp the message that this short book drives home. It is, in my opinion, a great read for anyone that has someone suffering from alcoholism in their lives."   Keith W.

"Daddy's Disease is a well written and informative book that manages to connect with kids of all ages. It addresses the feelings that so many kids of alcoholic parents have and helps them understand those feelings as well as understand alcoholism. I was impressed with how well the author was able to explain the disease of alcoholism in terms that a child can relate to. This book will help so many children deal with their feelings of hurt and confusion. A MUST read!"   Suzanne K.

"This is a "spot on" book for children of alcoholics. I had a Daddy Disease, so you can relate. More people than not need to read this book."   Maddie L.

"Carolyn Hannan Bell has captured the heart of children in a way that few can. Her insight to a child's confusion when living with alcoholism is incredibly valuable as she touches on issues that many adults fear to tread. Carolyn's ability to see into the heart of a child is nothing less than phenomenal. This is the most effective tool I have ever read when dealing with children and their understanding of alcoholism."
Monty Dale Meyer, CEO, Take 12 Recovery Radio * KHLT Recovery Broadcasting

Carolyn's webpage: www.alcoholismhurtskids.com

Made in the USA
San Bernardino, CA
02 February 2018